If your friends come to play,
what do you say?

Hello!

If someone gives you something nice,
what do you say?

Thank you!

If things go wrong while you're having fun, what do you say?

Sorry!

If you would like something,
what do you say?

Please!

If that sneeze takes you by surprise,
what do you say?

If you make a naughty noise,
what do you say?

Pardon!

If it's just a great big treat,
what do you say?

Hurray!

If someone is cheating,
what do you say?

Play fair!

If you leave a horrid mess,
what do you say?

Tidy up time!

When your party comes to an end,
what do you say?

Remember please and thank you too,

and lots of hugs will come to you!

to Jayne and the Bump!

A Red Fox Book: 0 09 943333 8

First published in Great Britain in 2003 by Red Fox
an imprint of Random House Children's Books

3 5 7 9 10 8 6 4

Red Fox Books are published by Random House Children's Books,
61-63 Uxbridge Road, London W5 5SA,
a division of The Random House Group, Ltd.

THE RANDOM HOUSE GROUP Limited Reg. No. 954009
www.kidsatrandomhouse.co.uk

A CIP catalogue record for this book is available from the British Library.

Printed and bound in Singapore